New York Revery

David Francis

ISBN: 978-81-19228-97-3

First Edition: 2023
Rs. 200/-

Cyberwit.net
HIG 45 Kaushambi Kunj, Kalindipuram
Allahabad - 211011 (U.P.) India
http://www.cyberwit.net
Tel: +(91) 9415091004
E-mail: info@cyberwit.net

Printed at Repro India Limited.

Acknowledgments

Big City Lit: "The Task"

The Brownstone Poets Anthology: "Xando" (2014), "Stereoscope Card" (2022)

Carillon: "Bowery"

Down in the Dirt: "Sole Revelation"

Eskimo Pie: "Inbal"

Fire: "Stop"

First Literary Review-East: "The Young Couple," "Quatrains (Section X)"

Indian Periodical: "My Companion," "It Was What I'd Hoped"

Ink Sweat & Tears: "Homage to Reznikoff"

Literary Yard: "Sound Man," "Notion"

Möbius, The Poetry Magazine: "The Songwriter"

The Recusant: "Van of Juveniles"

River Poets Journal: "Double Life"

The Screech Owl: "The Building"

Setu: "Quatrains (Section XII)," "Heart Song"

Snakeskin: "The Devil's Song," "Aesthetic Manners"

StepAway Magazine: "Enlivened Ghosts" (as "Meatpacking District, New York")

Voices on the Wind: "Spot," "Şafak," "Strange Lives"

Whisper: "Neon," "Elegy for an Actor," "Degradation of Bread"

W-Poesis: "When I Put Off the Bureaucratic Office," "Interval," "Artist-Animals," "The Contrast"

Contents

The Songwriter

I went back looking for my old Times Square
but my restaurant wasn't there
and my hotel wasn't there

only the numbered streets and the rivers

the trees were there and the glass complexes
the feeling of making the blocks but shrunken

my memory confronting actuality
met its match
there was nothing to grasp
there was no one to ask

Where was the basket of bread,
the bowl of soup, the strong coffee,
the blueberry pie with brown homemade crust?

Where was the old man behind the screen
in the lobby who said to my guitar,
"Are you going to play that thing?"

Where were the pigeons?
Where were the sills?
Where was the corner
my room looked out on,
the parking lot, the streetlight,

where was the cold water,
the sickly green paint, the jammed window,

the dresser lined with newspaper,
the phone covered in dust
which rang abruptly, faintly,
to leave a message?

Where was the clientele of
the excellent reasonably-priced
restaurant?
Where was the fresh produce
trucked in from New Jersey daily?

They must have all gone back where they came from.

The buildings seemed boarded up
but weren't;

but they had no life to them anymore,
no breathing stoops.

Where was the bum who demanded change
after I lit his cigarette?

Where was the lady who cursed
each passerby and when one turned
shut up?

Where were the alleys?

The sidewalks were the same.

Where was the plaza
where the truant kids hung out?

Where was the open entrance
of my hotel,
the sideways-hung sign
of my restaurant?

Stop

Stopped daydreaming
motionless traveling
through the car window staring
the woman's figure slumping
against the column standing
the human form expressing
the music hearing
before seeing
the saxophonist playing

today reading
suddenly realizing
precisely what missing
etched-held in waiting

the train moving
your train passengering
the beggar approaching

Spot

No one is listening.
He stares outside at the street,
remembering lyrics
by conditioned reflex.

He looks up at the clock
in a not too subtle way.

But he has a partner
who prompts him, offstage,
yet he, neither, is prepared:
so he hangs his head
and knits his brow
under his African hat
and strums the chords
over and over.

Monday night.

A single
in the tip basket.

The Building

The building is beautiful when pointed out to you. You noticed it alone. It takes up a block. Approached from the corner or the other side of the avenue, it's breathtaking. In the light of an early Sunday morning, when it stands naked and unappreciated beyond the deserted pavement, it monopolizes the sky. The archway, the columns, the bas-reliefs, the overwhelming detail of its façade enervate with their grandeur. The cornice, painted pewter, abuts the earth tones of the rest.

You do not storm it. You do not try to capture it. You do not bid to buy it. You do not impress it. You merely exclaim.

Later, after a long sleep, you sit at the tin counter of the deli, watching the rain, with the image of this building floating through your mind, with the memory of this building in its living coma.

Şafak

She comes up the street early
and hands me a cassette
of Turkish pop music, says
she will finish her poem
and bring it to me in a week.
Does she want to sit alone? Yes.

She pauses in the doorway
and fixes me with a puzzled look,
for I'm looking at her longingly;
the picture window shows her going by,
she just left with another guy:
this is the end of Sunday.

Give me a piece of the puzzle
give me an icebreaker
find me a locksmith
that I can unlock her heart with
make me a copy of the key

My mood is mean and surly,
I come close to getting in a fight;
"Man, we shouldn't get uptight
over a girl," he says, "she's just a bar girl."
She didn't fend off his affections;
I can't deal with this rejection.

Even though she is dusky
she shows up one day relaxed and tanned,

like someone who got out of New York City.
Where did she go? Puerto Rico.
“Oh, I have a gift for you,” and puts
a book of Spanish poems in my hand.

Give me a piece of the puzzle
give me an icebreaker
find me a locksmith
that I can unlock her heart with
make me a copy of the key

Enlivened Ghosts

Walk through this dead town
for years to come,
the ghosts are here haunting
the natives—
familial ghosts that
fuss and bother—
but I have my own
personal ghost
from a room
on 47th Street,
more spirit-like for
being bulldozed

a fly in the web
of memory
spun by the spider
of frustration,
I struggle, I sit tight
and I catch
through cataracts
glimpses of sunlight

something to do with
the waterfront:
a few blocks of
cobblestone markets
where old ferns drape
the unused trestle
and graffiti is scrawled
from times past

The Devil's Song

Crazed by grief and desire
and sticking his hand in the fire—
or was it ice?; he got frostbite:
the devil is beating his wife tonight.

Please I don't think I can go on,
I was somewhere else until the dawn—
still, there was an expanse and there was light
and I wasn't beating my wife last night.

Be forewarned: people will talk,
I said to the devil during our walk,
but out of mind, gossips are out of sight
and I'll neglect beating my wife tonight.

But now I am going through a mood swing,
I feel restless, like having a go at a fling;
this panic attack is giving me a fright
so I'm back to beating my wife tonight.

I'll walk home in the drizzle, lonely and tired,
but stop off at a café, I'm too wired
and all I can do is what I'm good at—not what's right:
my nature is beating my wife tonight.

Xando

Gabrielle looks out at the rainy weather
and eats a sandwich from off the counter;
she wants to slim down but her genes won't let her;
she's pale, she just needs a little sunshine.

Carmen came here to be a dancer;
now she's on the floor as a waitress trainer
and her eyes tear up but I don't have the answer:
she has her ambition and I have mine.

Eddy wants to make it as a singer;
as for lucky breaks, he needs a humdinger
but until he books at a faster pace
he's walking dogs over on Astor Place.

I sit, nursing their weak espresso,
stare dully at the rain beads on my face—
headlights search and whoosh, red green lights dayglow—
worried that someone must know the deadline
for all of us who are here in limbo.

When I Put Off the Bureaucratic Office

When I put off the bureaucratic office
I have a queasy feeling of guilt
like a penumbra hanging over me
a moist rotting toadstool
like an anchor of a weight of sand
and rain in a beached rowboat
like an unassuaged pain
of an unexplained disease
when I start off for the bureaucratic office
on a sunny day of melting snow
and icy air
I make stalwart drudging progress
like a barge watched from a
picture window on the Sound
I push the doors, hold them, show my ID
with an authoritarian flourish and I am there
and I wait but do not have to wait long
for I have a breezy purposeful aplomb
and I try to go around, like a pinball,
the dour faces and pitfall obstacle-cogs
to head toward an intelligent useful face
there is usually one (even in hell)
who will dispatch me in a painless manner

Neon

Impossibly thin—
walking down Sixth Avenue,
ancient, arm in arm,
bundled up for December:
she, eating a candy bar.

Sound Man

I go to the shows
no one knows
I cock my head
and bend my ear
I'm interested
in making the sound clear

I listen to the mix
it's my job to fix
the instruments I blend
the vocals I adjust
I'm the band's best friend
in me they trust

Turn up the mic
turn down the guitar
something's buzzing, like
hey man, I'm a star

They do not realize
from my point of view
this is just a disguise
I'm a musician too

but then after the show
who comes up but
the punk girl
and she says I
am the best
sound man
in the world

Interval

Feeling the raindrops
on my head absentmindedly,
dazed by a concern,
the streets, time, the world
that the browsing bookstore
was a refuge from…
the books from the past
that I once read in another language,
that I still could read, howbeit rusty…
a monastery peace
where the sacrifices of a life-choice
tug-of-war between the factions
of I don't know what…

No fair, I am tired like an
old man, exhausted
and yet, I believe
this state of defying the body
is key…

On the corner,
catching my reflection in the glass
with the displayed books:
where am I? My bag.
Feeling raindrops. Why?
I have forgotten.

A step back through
the open entrance,

summoning all my powers,
in the ravages of emotion
like a mouth trying to speak
through a dense cloth gag
I focus on “blue”
and, needing more, full-length—
not the word merely the shape
perception, like an animal—
and I pluck it dripping
from the umbrella pail.

Notion

Far away
maybe I could have loved her
if I had stayed
maybe I'll go back one day

A lost love
maybe I could have found peace
in her like a dove
we could have fit like a glove

you never know
maybe we could have loved each other
even though
different yet familiar
what could have been
is put off till tomorrow

one day one-way of flying
maybe back one day to stay
or maybe I'll just keep sighing
with this daydream so unsatisfying

Le Weekend (Esperanto Café)

In the café crowded to capacity,
SRO with espresso,
a blonde face looms, "Dude,
if you want to sit down
we'll move to the sofa…"
a quartet of girls conversing,
hilarious, the leader
about "counterculture," another,
less patrician, censuring
"I am not an extremist!"
the giggling one blowing out
a Chinese finger trap like a
party favor, from religion
to borrowing shoes, changing
patterns in their shared kaleidoscope
but when two go off to the rest room:
"If you don't like me the way I am—"
smiling belying the drizzle
outside of Ha ha that's so funny
Ha Saturday night!

The Young Couple

They hardly look at each other
but they are in each other's mind
their faces are beatific
shine like old movie close-ups

the tall gangly boy
holds the short stockier girl
both the same age, the same freshness

you mustn't stare at them
as though disturbingly aware
of something forgotten

even though
the swan on the river
and the dogwood blossom
are suddenly in their faces
like a magic mirror.

Illusions of Mirrors

On a mirror
on the bricks
high above
the upright piano
slanted down gives
a blonde face
in the elbow
of the gilt-framed
mirror on the
opposite wall

Strange Lives

She lives with a man who stays up all night,
sleeps in between his two rooms burning bright,
shares his moods and hours spent waiting to write;

and the years pass on their seasonal rounds:
old music, their voices, the traffic sounds
inhabit their world of nuptial bounds;

and displayed are the photos on the wall,
all the epochs hagiographical,
the personal empire, its rise and fall.

What is strange, though, in the still of the night
is how fate has chosen thus to alight,
scaring like pigeons all options to flight;

for though the earth has its dull constancy—
night following day, again, endlessly—
human wills fluctuate like the economy;

given this, the reasons may be virtues
that cement her continuing to choose
the lighted room with its dark window views.

Artist-Animals

Like people in cages,
you come to see us eat,
you are afraid of our teeth
and our claws,
you let us breathe
but when we pause—
out of the terrible fatalism
of these walls—
to rest or sleep, as is our wont,
you mock and taunt
us, give catcalls,
stare at us with cruel thirsty eyes
from your stolid bulks
(like a fold of fatty flesh, you
are, alas, our window view):
you want us to jig on one leg,
to be cute, to beg,
and we wait for the closing hour,
last call for your barbarism
the ticket-price empowers
for the peanuts and coins you toss
at (in your dreams) your lordly boss—
cursing us when, yawning, nonchalant,
we roll over and swat at fleas...

Quatrains

I

Pretend like we're having fun—
pretend like we're studying—
it isn't children who pretend
but Adults playacting.

II

We are all these wayward children
and we never did grow up
and all we have is a dog-eared paperback
and a refill in the coffee cup

III

The atmosphere in here is so thick
you could cut it with a knife,
and these…people are so rigid
they are more deathlike than life-

IV

Don't nail anything in rotten timber
don't marry a gold-digger for love
and if you leave hell please don't reenter
and if you see heaven know that it's enough

V

Each involved in his own activity;
the urgency of the event is lame:
a bunch of islands having a party
made of hollow shells and the sounding sea.

VI

I look at the world in openmouthed surprise
and see how superficial it is with my X-ray eyes
and it seems as though the nice people stay inside
and the ones who had hope fall by the wayside

VII

If I can't voyage into the unknown
then I know I won't avoid a stale fate
in a cedar chest smelling of mothballs,
a product beyond its expiration date.

VIII

Somewhere someone is sticking pins
in an effigy
the cure's amnesia
the disease is memory

IX

The people snoring and the rain falling,
the silent steps, pregnant with sound, go down

with the timbers and the oldness calling:
the prison of night, a provincial town.

X

What is a desire? It keeps you hanging
over the chasm. The ground you stand on
has been washed away by the waves banging
until the whole sea-facing cliff is gone.

XI

As long as you have a shield against the foe
as long as you have a coat against the wind
and of that shield and of that coat you
never let go
because in this world there is not one true
friend

XII

The ghost of the young traveler within,
I tried but couldn't get lost in the crowd;
was it that I had outgrown the City
or was it that I'd outgrown my own skin?

XIII

Music has cured me
as silence has cured me;
but certainly one of the two
will come to the rescue.

SLAP SLAP

a dialogue of two young Irish women

Slap slap
you get one slap
he gets another one
know what I mean

move along quickly

I said
and I was like

while you felt
that you were still seeing each other

that's when I said
and he's like
if you're going away
well I'm sorry
but when you come back
we can still be friends
well he said I told you
and even if he said
well we can still be friends

well how do you feel

I dunno

he has a point
he has a black-and-white point
to be honest

well that's the reason
that he pulled away
big time

how does she feel

how would you feel

you're just gonna suck it up

she I'm telling you
she ended it

you've just got to decide
what you're gonna do here
you shouldn't feel that bad

well basically
but back to the original conversation
knowing now

that would've crushed me
I can see why you didn't mention it
that's embarrassing

well there you go
a little eye-opener

not that person
and it takes a while to get over that
and I guarantee if you knew

didn't want to know
but I did want to
you do it's natural
to be perfectly honest

I would grab her by the hair
and hold her there
would you believe it

with that kind of situation
you've just gotta hold back

but don't play games
that's childish
and if he did it's even worse

so there I was
thinking I was gettin' somewhere
let's face it

I see right through it
you've got the high ground

Double Life

He fell asleep on Essex Street
where he sat in the driver's seat
of the car service vehicle—
not a very safe place to sleep
with the windows up, oblivious,
dog-tired in the summertime heat
(maybe he held two or three jobs).
Where is the time for forty winks
within twenty-four-seven weeks?

On the same dirty city street—
the smells of oil and car exhaust—
wondering what stranger he might meet,
so much better off than before
when he knew no one save in dreams,
broke, with tenuous connections
like a blinking bulb in a lamp,
the day after a performance:
should he escape or hatch a plot?

Bowery

In the Chinese movie
I want to leave early
but in my row
sits an old man
with a cane,
in front of him
a young man asleep,
his head back—
this narrow passage
I decide to eschew.

Sole Revelation

Some days you realize you are wounded
as crippled as the wheelchair man
you are as twisted as a wrought-iron spear
and have only the wind to straighten it
this is you, take it or leave it
overcast or sunny: one afternoon
you have this sole revelation

Aesthetic Manners

There has to be some orthodoxy
whose mask issues from insecurity:
the filmmaker assures his crony,
"It's a documentary—but crazy..."
not to be bridled with solemnity,
the past taboo: class in society
was beaten down by this barbarity—
of this leveling conformity
only the bum or genius is free.

Heart Song

She turned so soft and so weak
like a feather, fallen,
with a pulse, so to speak,
as when we were together
but floating from that peak

Lunatic at the Horseshoe Counter

This lunatic
is tolerated
though anyone
who sits near him
will consider himself
ill-fated—
this is guaranteed:
if your leisure is of any worth,
give him a wide berth;
he breaks into a screed
in a nonstop metallic
voice that comments on
some news item he has happened to read,
surrealistically mixed with general…
such is his shtick—
strangers may fear him,
pretend not to hear him
but to the wait staff who matter
he's no persona non grata
and, never turned away,
comes in once a day,
a real habitué
of the fashionable café
where he drinks…water,
never ordering food,
which, word-competing, wouldn't be chewed;
he has one other mood:
that is euphoria
over euphony and rhythm;

he always brings a CD player
with his fresh newspaper;
dancing in his seat
to the beat
of the unheard invisible score—to you.

The Task

Three girls placing long-stemmed roses in a vase
placing and re-placing them in a frenzy
in the clear vase of visible compressed leaves
until you can't tell if they're putting or pulling
they are so rapt in this dizzying pastime
which they were born for, their joy of arrangement
rendering them as one with the flowers they admire,
tight-wrapped petals of pink and yellow

The Contrast

The contrast
above the dark windowless cornice
of the smoke billowing
with the night sky
that the penthouse abuts
so emptily;
on the terrarium a fir
is visible
up above
the scaffolding
and the avenues
and all the people
and all their mundane glamor
which makes tired eyes seek
the reality
of the fantastical shapes,
arabesques, curlicues
and chimney effusions
of the thick, mercurial,
remote and enigmatical
smoke.

A

Yes, it's brutally cold today
but at least it will clear the air,
it will blow the gloom away
that several days of drizzle put there:
now it's sunny on Avenue A.

Now a certain luminosity
attaches to figures like a kind of peach fuzz;
before, a vague viscosity
oppressed both hue and contour: blues were blahs
and the skyline was an atrocity!

Opera booms in the café
and through the plate glass
crisp leaves pirouette a ballet
and trash papers make a mad exodus
to Tompkins Square Park across Avenue A.

O spread you great splotch-trunked tree,
stand you brown tenement in such blue air;
it's true that pedestrians walk briskly,
hunchbacked, intent on getting somewhere
but lo, what matters is the journey

not the destination anyway:
ski masks, gloves, red ears, cold tears
ripped from the eyes
are the price you pay
for the vanishing point on the horizon
down the straight line of Avenue A.

In the Park at Dawn

Peach light
on the façades,
a bag
left on the bench,
its ownership tag blank;

serrated leaves
over the paths,
a squirrel nose-dives,
claw-holds bark,
munching an acorn,

falls; pigeons peck
in the garden
and birds squeal
in the distance;

look closely at the
grassless banks of the path:
bottle caps, butts, foil,
a solitary ant
on a scrag of driftwood

Inbal

Inbal, Inbal,
the first time
I saw you
you had
panache;
what you had
made me
wish to lose
control:
one cold glance
from you
could my hopes
annul.

Then one night
you came
to see me
perform;
you were part
of our
entourage
patrol;
you stayed
without my
having to
cajole.

Another night
we went

to a
saloon;
you filled in
the facts
of your
foreign soul;
we rated
New York,
pros and cons
and all:
I wondered
what ever
could be
my role.

Wanderlust
we shared
by common
consent:
South America
looming as
your goal.

Then your friend
said you
had left town
for good.

I see you on
the other platform,
Inbal...
in your fur coat

waving away
you stole.

Separate-bound
trains no
one can
console.

My Companion

Please don't rank on my guitar
she has taken me this far
I don't care who you are

it's OK if you say she's old
because she's vintage so I'm told
but don't ask her age don't be that bold

to ooh and aah that she's rare
is fine say she's beyond compare
but don't ask how she "frets up there"

or if her action's high or low
it's none of your business you know
she's rather temperamental so…

And if she goes off
          out of tune
needing constant attention
what she gives is worth
                    much more
than lesser lights
          can mention

I Saw a Man

I saw a guy
he was middle-aged
his nerves were shot
his hair was gray

what kind of society is this
maybe it was drugs that made him blissed
maybe it's just hit or miss

it's quantity over quality
everybody's a casualty
why does this have to be

people are pieces
of a machine
the looks on the faces
are steely and mean

it's just like *Metropolis*

this song isn't very nice
but I don't care
all I'm doing is telling the truth
I swear

you don't have to applaud or hiss
if you can't take the tragedy

Homage to Reznikoff

In a cold spot
behind the garden
to the all-night café
the snow remains:
it doesn't mean
snow will blanket
the sidewalk all the way
to the station;
it will remain, unseen
by the Sunday sleepers.

Elegy for an Actor

Well, Viktor is dead
and he will speak no more,
he who was an actor
and imitated the dead,
throwing back his head
with a lack of snore.

He was hammy, needy,
he was vulnerable,
he was selfish and uncaring,
he was gullible:
this is what I'd've said
at his funeral.

But there's something more.
He was in your face
like the old New York:
he never slept and he could talk,
he could carve it with a knife,
he could dish it out with a fork
and take it by the score;
but his own peculiar life—
no one will take his place.

Van of Juveniles

Some “juveniles” just went by in a van,
their faces so dark in the night darkness,
and they looked at me and I looked at them
huddled, guarded, indistinct, in transit;
myself at an outdoor café table
spot-lit, and them waiting for the red light.

Their chief problem, like ours, is to kill time
but we are outside, free, oblivious;
they are like the inert scattered leaves of fall,
dark-bound for the prison population,
the great waste of the undeclared empire,
the kept secret that I share among them.

But if you have ever been a teacher
you resent them and care for them much more
than you can admit to, in your comfort,
because they are part of your suffering
from the same target of hypocrisy,
the same angry arrow missing its mark.

Stereoscope Card

For a time that never was
but the acorns fallen then
still fall. The trees were and are in bloom!
The mimosa's inexpressible.
You may catch a whiff of mothballs
on a hurrying street, or from a cedar chest
in memory.

Maurice Utrillo on the wall
a telephone with which to call
a leaking faucet

An old couple with patched violin cases
stepping off
a city bus at noon in Manhattan.

I saw *The Persistence of Memory*
and wondered at how small it was;
unlike the illustration in art books
you could see the brushstrokes.

For a time
when the crowd sat under the trees;
Lyonel Feininger sailing boats
with his son
on the reservoir in Central Park.

Nobody laughed at the Dadaists;
they took them too seriously, solemnly,
they didn't get the joke.

Marc Chagall did his murals
for the Metropolitan Opera House
but never really liked New York
and went back to his beloved Paris.

I went around the wall and there was
Guernica

Degradation of Bread

The old wife calls
                    down the length of the sidewalk;
his back to us,
                he walks on;
again she calls—
then the deliveryman yells "Hey!";
the old man turns, waits;
his wife makes up the distance:
"I called you."
"I didn't hear you;
I'm going to get a—"
obscured by the street noise;

she walks through the pigeons
he was feeding from his chair
(which he does every day)
and kicks the hard loaf
like a football
again and again
until it lies in the street
and is then lifted
by the plunging beaks.

It Was What I'd Hoped

I got up late
looked out the window
it was the dark of wintertime
but it wasn't snowing
I skipped breakfast
next walked straight to my café
and pulled your airmail letter
out of my attaché
and trying not to tear the return address
I hurriedly tore it into shreds
not letting the world interlope
focused on finding out if
what you wrote was what I hoped

Twenty years have passed
and sometimes I wonder if this will be the last
before drifting to sleep
I suffer pangs of remorse
I see myself a failure
a shipwrecked sailor
how did I arrive on this island
what wind twisted my course
what happened to that siren
can you find it in your heart
to overlook the wasted years
with which I cannot cope
but it's just déjà vu
a cycle we go through
revolving like a gyroscope

twenty years' time at a standstill
how I get the same thrill
as back then when I saw your envelope
and knew with absolute certainty
of love that it was what I'd hoped

The Promenade

oily majestic
twilight
water

against
subway tunnel
black

against
the railing
close cars
rushing below

wind
river ocean
mouth
welcoming

the
abandoned
vantage
dark open

as brilliant
tiers of traffic
blur

fade
as an old snapshot
behind you lost

www.ingramcontent.com/pod-product-compliance
Lightning Source LLC
LaVergne TN
LVHW101954220826
846093LV00006B/223